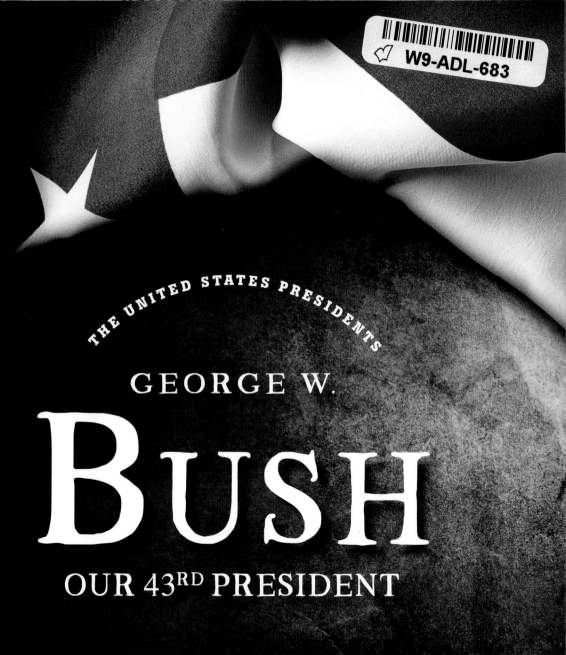

THE UNITED STATES PRESIDENTS

GEORGE W.

BUSH

OUR 43RD PRESIDENT

by Michael Burgan

The Child's World®
childsworld.com

1980 Lookout Drive • Mankato, MN 56003-1705
800-599-READ • www.childsworld.com

ACKNOWLEDGMENTS
Content Adviser: David R. Smith, Adjunct Assistant
Professor of History, University of Michigan–Ann Arbor

PHOTOS
Cover and page 3: Eric Draper, photographer, courtesy of the
George Bush Presidential Library (detail)
Interior: Associated Press, 4, 9, 15, 16, 26, 28, 29, 32, 33, 34, 38
(bottom left), 39; CHIP SOMODEVILLA/KRT/Newscom, 30; CHUCK
KENNEDY/KRT/Newscom, 27; COLIN BRALEY/REUTERS/Newscom, 20;
Gary Williams/ZUMAPRESS/Newscom, 35; GEORGE BRIDGES/KRT/
Newscom, 19; George H.W. Bush Presidential Library and Museum,
5, 6, 7, 8, 10, 14, 38 (top left and right); John Moore/MCT/Newscom,
36; Joseph Sohm/Shutterstock.com, 18; Peter Silva/ZUMAPRESS/
Newscom, 13; *The Palm Beach Post*/ZUMA Press/Newscom, 12; US
National Archives and Records Administration, 21, 23, 24; White
House/ZUMA Press/Newscom, 22; © 2000 William Coupon; National
Portrait Gallery, Smithsonian Institution; gift of William Coupon, 37

ISBN 9781503844346 (REINFORCED LIBRARY BINDING)
ISBN 9781503846944 (PORTABLE DOCUMENT FORMAT)
ISBN 9781503848139 (ONLINE MULTI-USER EBOOK)
LCCN 2019957754

Printed in the United States of America

CONTENTS

*George W. Bush served
as president from
2001 to 2009.*

CHAPTER ONE

PREPARING TO SERVE

As the 43rd president of the United States, George W. Bush had to deal with some very difficult issues. In the fall of 2000, he was elected in one of the closest presidential elections in US history. After only eight months in office, Bush was faced with guiding the country after deadly **terrorist** attacks on the World Trade Center and the Pentagon. Americans were furious at the attackers, a group called al-Qaeda, and wanted the leaders found. President Bush sent US troops to the country of Afghanistan, where the leaders of al-Qaeda were known to hide. Thus began what was called the war on terror. This war would dominate Bush's presidency.

When he became president, George W. Bush carried on a long family tradition of government service. His grandfather, Prescott Bush, was a US senator from Connecticut. Prescott's son, George H. W. Bush, became active in **politics** in the 1960s and was elected president in 1988.

George W. Bush in 2002

His son, George W., helped in that **campaign.** In many ways, the younger Bush followed in his father's footsteps.

George H. W. Bush and his wife, Barbara Pierce Bush, lived in New Haven, Connecticut, when George W. was born on July 6, 1946. The elder Bush had served as a navy pilot during World War II. He was awarded the Distinguished Flying Cross for bravery in action. After the war, he then went to New Haven to study at Yale University, one of the top colleges in the United States.

In 1948, the Bush family moved to Texas, where George H. W. got a job with a company that sold equipment to the oil industry. Oil was big business in Texas. After a few years in Texas, Bush decided to start his own oil company.

The family settled in Midland, a town in West Texas. George W. spent a large part of his childhood there before the Bushes moved to Houston. In 1949, the Bushes had a daughter named Robin. During the 1950s, the family grew to include four more children: Jeb, Neil, Marvin, and Dorothy. Robin died of cancer before her fourth birthday. Relatives said George W. tried to cheer up his parents.

In Texas, George W. attended both public and private schools. At the age of 15, he began attending Phillips Academy, a private high school in Andover, Massachusetts. His father had gone to the same school. A classmate recalled that George W. was "one of the cool guys" at the school.

George W. Bush played Little League baseball as a child. He developed a lifelong love for the game.

The Bush family is pictured in their home in Houston, Texas, in 1964—the year that George H. W. ran for the US Senate but lost. Two years later, he would be elected to the House of Representatives. Pictured from left to right are Marvin, George H. W., Dorothy, Jeb, Barbara, Neil, and George W.

In class, George W. struggled at first, but as he later wrote, "I buckled down, worked hard, and learned a lot."

In 1964, George W. graduated from Phillips Academy. He planned to enter Yale University in the fall. During the summer, he returned to Texas, where his father was beginning a campaign for the US Senate. The younger Bush rode a bus across the state, helping his father. George's father was generally **conservative.** He belonged to the Republican Party, one of the nation's two major **political parties.** Most Texans at the time belonged to the Democratic Party, and his father lost the election.

During his four years at Yale, George W. studied history and enjoyed reading. He also briefly played on the baseball team and learned how to play rugby.

While George W. Bush was at Yale, his father was elected to the US House of Representatives.

The years that George W. spent at Yale were sometimes difficult ones for the United States. The country was at war with **communist** forces in Vietnam, a country in Asia, and many college students protested the war. George W. did not agree with the protesters. He later called the 1960s "a confusing and disturbing time."

When George W. Bush left Yale in 1968, he joined the Texas Air **National Guard.** At the time, most people who joined the National Guard, including Bush, served in the United States rather than going to fight overseas. After 1970, Bush served part-time in the National Guard, while he worked for several Republican **candidates.**

At Phillips Academy, students sometimes played a type of baseball called stickball. George W. was named the head of the school's stickball league, a sign of his popularity with the other students.

George H. W. pins a lieutenant bar on his son, George W., in 1968, after he was made an officer in the Texas Air National Guard. George W. completed Air Force flight training and served as an F-102 fighter pilot until 1973.

George W. learned how to fly military jets while serving in the Texas Air National Guard.

In 1971, George W. Bush took his first full-time job. He began working for a Texas company that raised and produced food for farm animals. Bush called the position a "coat-and-tie job" and left after one year. For a time in 1972, he thought about running for the Texas **legislature,** but he decided he wanted to gain more experience before entering politics.

By this time, George H. W. Bush was the US **ambassador** to the **United Nations.** In that role, he met with ambassadors from around the world and tried to win support for US plans. US president Richard Nixon then asked the elder Bush to run the Republican Party. George H. W. Bush became one of the most important party members in the country.

George and Laura Bush were married in Midland, Texas, on November 5, 1977.

Although he was drawn to politics, George W. also thought about someday running his own company. In 1973, he entered Harvard University to study for an advanced degree in business. Bush was now a more serious student than he had been in high school and college, and he enjoyed his classwork. When he graduated in 1975, he returned to Texas to enter the oil business. He knew, he later wrote, "that if I worked hard and hustled I could make a living."

In 1981, George W. and Laura Bush's twin daughters, Barbara and Jenna, were born. Years later, Barbara continued the family tradition of attending college at Yale, while Jenna attended the University of Texas.

Bush did work hard and became successful. But he didn't lose his interest in politics. In 1977, he ran for the US Congress. That same year, he met Laura Welch, a school librarian in Houston. The two fell in love and married in November. With his campaign under way, Bush did not have time for a honeymoon. His first task was to beat other Republicans to win the party's **nomination.** He succeeded, but in the fall of 1978, he lost to the Democratic candidate.

In 1980, George H. W. Bush ran for the Republican presidential nomination. He lost to Ronald Reagan, but Reagan chose Bush as his vice presidential candidate. The younger Bush, his brothers, and his sister all worked for their father and Reagan during the campaign. In November, the Reagan-Bush team won the election. Four years later, Reagan and Bush won again. The younger Bush would soon become even more involved in politics.

A RELIGIOUS REBIRTH

In 1985, George W. Bush had a religious experience that changed his life. The Bushes had raised George W. in the Episcopal and Presbyterian churches. Later, he attended Methodist church services with his wife, Laura. "I had always been a religious person," he once wrote, but "my faith took on a new meaning" after a weekend with the Reverend Billy Graham (pictured above, preaching to a crowd in Florida in 1981).

Graham, one of the most famous ministers of the 20th century, sometimes preached in front of tens of thousands of people.

Graham gave Bush a new understanding of the Bible and Christian beliefs. Bush began to read the Bible regularly and discuss it with friends. He quit drinking alcohol. As president, Bush often talked about the important role his faith played in his life.

CHAPTER TWO

BUILDING A POLITICAL CAREER

During the early 1980s, George W. Bush continued his work at Arbusto Energy, which he later renamed Bush Exploration. At first, Bush did well in the oil business, but oil prices began to fall in the mid–1980s. This made it hard for oil companies to earn money. Arbusto Energy combined with another oil company, Spectrum 7, and Bush became chairman. Another company, Harken Energy, later bought Spectrum 7.

Meanwhile, George H. W. Bush began preparing for the 1988 presidential race. George W. played a major role in that campaign by helping his father win the support of conservative Christian voters. George W. Bush convinced many of these voters that his father would support their political interests.

George W. Bush served two terms as governor of Texas.

George and Laura Bush pose with their daughters, Barbara (left) and Jenna, in 1981 at Walker's Point, the Bush family's estate, in Kennebunkport, Maine.

In November 1988, George H. W. Bush won the presidency. Just before the new president and his wife settled into the White House, George W. moved into a new home in Dallas. Some journalists suggested George W. was thinking about running for governor in Texas. Some Texas Republicans felt it was too soon for him to run for office. One Republican leader even told George W. that he needed "to go out in the world and do something."

Meanwhile, George H. W. Bush worked hard at the difficult job of running the US government. His biggest challenge came in August 1990. Iraqi leader Saddam Hussein had ordered Iraqi troops to invade the neighboring country of Kuwait to seize control of its oil.

President Bush organized a military **coalition.** Early in 1991, coalition troops forced the Iraqi army out of Kuwait. Some Americans believed the coalition troops should have removed Saddam from power. President Bush said that he did not have the legal power to do so.

With the victory, almost 90 percent of Americans approved of President Bush's actions as president. But by the 1992 presidential election, that number fell sharply. Many voters questioned how Bush had handled the US economy. Many workers had lost their jobs. The president had also broken a promise he had made to not raise taxes. In November, Democrat Bill Clinton was elected the 42nd president. George W. later called 1992 "a long and miserable year."

In 1989, George W. Bush became part owner of the Texas Rangers baseball team. He represented the other owners in public and attended many of the games. He sold his share of the team in 1998.

First Lady Barbara Bush throws out a pitch before the start of a Texas Rangers baseball game in 1989. Her son George W. became an owner of the Texas Rangers that year.

George W. was not the only Bush child to enter politics. Jeb Bush started campaigning for Florida governor a few months before George W. entered the Texas race. Jeb lost the election, but in 1998 he ran again and won. Jeb served as governor of Florida from 1999 to 2007. In 2016, Jeb campaigned to be the Republican presidential nominee, but he lost the nomination to Donald Trump.

The following year, George W. announced he was running for governor of Texas. The current governor was Democrat Ann Richards, who was well liked in the state. Some of Bush's advisers did not think he could win a campaign against the popular governor. They felt people did not know enough about him. Bush, however, was confident that he could win. As the son of a former US president, people knew the Bush family and what they believed in.

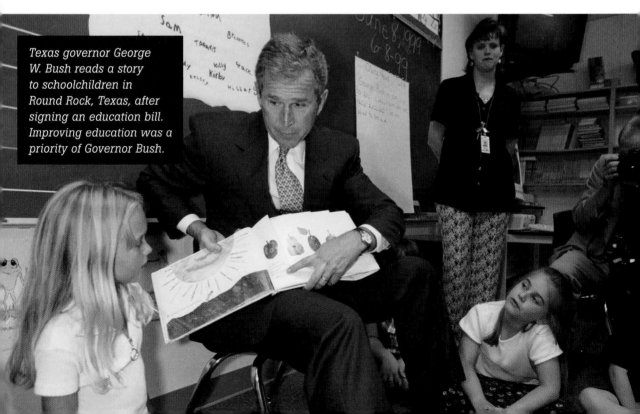

Texas governor George W. Bush reads a story to schoolchildren in Round Rock, Texas, after signing an education bill. Improving education was a priority of Governor Bush.

George W. was not always comfortable making speeches. He was at his best when he met voters in small groups. He talked about reducing crime and improving education. He also wanted to help the owners of small businesses. In November 1994, Bush defeated Richards.

Bush was only the second Republican governor of Texas in more than 120 years. He had to work closely with Democratic lawmakers. He was able to win their support many times. He cut taxes and toughened jail sentences for criminals. He also reformed the **welfare system.** Bush wanted people who received government aid to find jobs or go to school so they could learn new skills. His goal was to get people off welfare. In 1988, Bush easily won reelection.

George W. Bush always believed it was important to be on time for public events. As a candidate and politician, he usually arrived early— sometimes even before reporters and TV cameras reached the event. Bush's aides often told him to drive around the block so the reporters had time to prepare for his arrival.

After his victory, Bush said, "My compassionate conservative philosophy is making Texas a better place." Bush had been calling himself a compassionate conservative for more than a year. That meant that he held conservative views, such as limiting the powers of government and promoting business growth. At the same time, he believed government should help people when they truly needed it.

Even before Bush won his reelection, he was thinking about running for president. President Bill Clinton had won a second term as president in 1996, and Vice President Al Gore was likely to be the Democratic presidential candidate in 2000. By 1999, Bush was meeting with Republican Party advisers to learn more about important issues. He also started raising money. Running for president is expensive, because candidates must travel across the country and buy ads to communicate their views. Bush eventually raised more than $100 million for his campaign. Bush won the Republican nomination for president and chose Dick Cheney as his vice presidential candidate. Al Gore was the Democratic candidate.

During the campaign, Bush continued to spread his message of compassionate conservatism. He supported a new program that would give religious organizations a larger role in the government's efforts to help

troubled people. Bush also wanted to cut taxes and spend more money on the US military. Bush hoped to end arguments between Republicans and Democrats. He pointed out that he had worked well with Democrats in Texas. Bush told the nation, "I am a uniter, not a divider."

The 2000 presidential election was one of the closest in US history. On Election Day, Gore won more total votes, or the popular vote. Bush, however, won more **electoral votes.**

Dick Cheney was working as a businessman when he became the Republican candidate for vice president.

George W. Bush takes the oath of office during his inauguration as the 43rd president of the United States, as his wife, Laura, and daughters stand beside him. Because of the problems encountered with voting machines in Florida, the election results were not settled until several weeks after Election Day.

Each state has as many electoral votes as its combined total of US senators and US representatives. In most states, the winner of the popular vote receives all of that state's electoral votes. It doesn't matter whether the candidate won by one vote or a million votes. Because of this, the winner of the national popular vote does not always win the national electoral vote.

Though Election Day was November 7, 2000, the final results of the election were delayed for almost six weeks because of voting problems in Florida. The entire election hinged on who won the vote in Florida. After much arguing, Bush was declared the winner of the national election by just one electoral vote.

On January 20, 2001, George W. Bush was sworn in as the 43rd president of the United States. The nation looked on as he promised to preserve, protect, and defend the US **Constitution.** At his **inauguration,** Bush said he wanted to end the hostility between Republicans and Democrats sparked by the close vote in Florida. He hoped members of both parties would "come together and do what's right for America."

THE FLORIDA VOTE OF 2000

The 2000 election in Florida had many problems. Some registered voters found that their names were not on the list of legal voters. In some counties, ballots were so confusing that people accidentally voted for the wrong candidate. And in some places, the voting machines did not read the votes that had been cast. In the photo above, people protest outside of the courthouse in Palm Beach County, Florida, over ballots they said were confusing and misleading.

By the end of Election Day, Bush was ahead of Gore by a few thousand votes. The election was so close that, under Florida law, the votes had to be recounted before state officials could declare a winner.

The recount process ended up in court, as both sides argued about which ballots should be counted. The legal battle finally went to the US Supreme Court, the most powerful court in the country. Gore and the Democrats wanted more time for a recount of about 9,000 votes cast in one South Florida county. But on December 12 the Supreme Court declared that the recount had to stop. They said it was unconstitutional to continue to count the votes in only one county, instead of the entire state. As a result, the original recount stood. Bush won the state by slightly more than 500 votes out of more than 6 million cast.

CHAPTER THREE

AMERICA AT WAR

As his presidency began, Bush focused on **domestic** issues. The US economy had weakened, and some people had lost their jobs. As he had promised, Bush asked Congress to pass a huge tax cut. Bush's plan involved giving taxpayers more money to save for the future. They could also spend the money, which would help companies that make products. Those companies could then hire more workers. To help businesses further, he ended some government rules that made doing business more expensive.

Bush also dealt with international issues. He called for the development of a new missile defense system to protect the country. He wanted a system in which missiles would be shot down in space, before they reached the United States. In 1972, the United States had signed a **treaty** saying it would not build this kind of missile system. Bush argued that protecting America was more important than honoring the treaty.

George W. Bush dealt with many difficult issues during his presidency.

George W. Bush shares a laugh with his father while sitting at the president's desk for the first time.

He also pulled out of another treaty designed to limit air pollution. In 1997, the United States had agreed to limit the production of certain gases that harm the environment. Bush decided that following the treaty would be too costly for US businesses, and that those costs would eventually be passed on to consumers as price increases. Many of Bush's decisions angered Democrats. They thought Bush was breaking his promise to work with them and be a "uniter."

But many Democrats joined with the president to try to improve US schools. Bush called this effort No Child Left Behind. He wanted students to be tested regularly to make sure they were learning what they were supposed to learn. Parents could move their children to better schools if the test scores at their current schools were too low.

Education, taxes, and the environment are all issues vital to the United States. But after September 11, 2001, a new concern arose that would dominate the rest of George W. Bush's presidency. That day, the nation came under attack. Terrorists **hijacked** four planes and used them as missiles to strike important buildings. Two of the planes crashed into the twin towers of the World Trade Center in New York City. Another struck the Pentagon, the headquarters for the US military. A fourth crashed in a field in Pennsylvania. Almost 3,000 people died in the attacks.

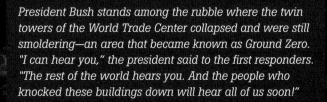

President Bush stands among the rubble where the twin towers of the World Trade Center collapsed and were still smoldering—an area that became known as Ground Zero. "I can hear you," the president said to the first responders. "The rest of the world hears you. And the people who knocked these buildings down will hear all of us soon!"

A group called al-Qaeda had carried out the attacks. Osama bin Laden, a man from the Middle Eastern nation of Saudi Arabia, was the leader of al-Qaeda. He and his supporters belonged to an extreme branch of the religion of Islam. They stated in writing and videos that their motivations for the attacks included oppression of and attacks against Muslims, as well as US support for Israel and the presence of US troops in Saudi Arabia, among other things. Bin Laden shared these views with the Taliban, a group that led Afghanistan at the time.

Bush struck back at al-Qaeda by sending troops into Afghanistan, where bin Laden was hiding. In October 2001, US planes streaked over Afghanistan. Military troops from other countries joined the battle, as did Afghan forces that opposed the Taliban. Within two months, the **allies** had forced the Taliban from power. Bin Laden, however, was still on the loose in the rugged mountains between Afghanistan and Pakistan.

US Navy fighter aircraft armed with missiles patrol the skies over Afghanistan in November 2001 during Operation Enduring Freedom, the US government's response to the September 11 terrorist attacks.

In January 2002, President Bush named Iraq, North Korea, and Iran as the major nations that helped terrorists. He called them "an axis of evil."

President Bush next turned his attention to Iraq. Bush and his advisers had long considered Saddam Hussein a major threat. They feared he had **weapons of mass destruction** (WMDs) and might give them to terrorists to use against the United States. But some experts, even within the US government, did not believe Iraq had WMDs.

Throughout 2002, Bush spoke to Americans, explaining that attacking Iraq was a key part of the war on terror. Meanwhile, officials from the United Nations (UN) were searching for WMDs in Iraq. UN rules required that Saddam Hussein give up all his WMDs. UN teams had already been searching there for a long time. Some US lawmakers wanted the hunt for WMDs to stop, while others wanted to give the UN more time to complete its search. In the end, Congress gave Bush the authority to invade Iraq.

Most other nations did not agree with Bush's approach in Iraq. Only Great Britain committed a large number of troops to the effort. Even close US allies such as Canada did not join the coalition.

In March 2003, Bush told Saddam Hussein that he had 48 hours to leave the country. If he refused, the United States would attack. Hussein claimed, as he had before, that Iraq did not have WMDs. Was he telling the truth? Hussein was a leader who had murdered and lied to gain power in his country. Could he be trusted now?

George W. Bush's father, George H. W. Bush, was the 41st US president. But the Bushes were not the first father and son to have both held the office. John Adams became the second US president in 1797. His son, John Quincy Adams, became the sixth president in 1825.

On March 19, US military forces invaded Iraq. Within four weeks, the United States and its allies had taken Baghdad, the Iraqi capital, and forced Saddam Hussein from power. On May 1, Bush said major fighting was over in Iraq. But he warned it would take some time to bring peace and **democracy** to Iraq. In the months that followed, Iraqi **insurgents** began attacking US forces. As the months passed, the attacks became more and more common.

Meanwhile, US forces never found WMDs in Iraq. Some Americans felt that the president had lied about Iraq having WMDs. They thought he had used them as an excuse to get rid of Saddam Hussein. They thought Bush had started a war unnecessarily. Bush argued that it was good to remove Hussein even if he did not have WMDs because he had been a brutal ruler who often killed and tortured his own people.

US soldiers patrol a Baghdad neighborhood in 2003. More than 200,000 Americans took part in the invasion of Iraq.

Senator John Kerry of Massachusetts was the Democratic candidate for president in 2004. He began serving in the Senate in 1985.

In 2004, Bush ran for a second term as president. His popularity had fallen since September 2001. Some Americans questioned his decision to invade Iraq. Others did not like his tax cuts and believed the economy was suffering. Bush argued that his efforts would add new jobs in the years to come. He also said he was the best person to lead the country's war on terror.

Bush's opponent in 2004 was Senator John Kerry of Massachusetts. Kerry had won several medals during the Vietnam War. During the campaign, he spoke often about his war record. He said his experience would make him a good military leader. Yet he also believed in using **diplomacy.** He attacked Bush for not trying hard enough to avoid a war in Iraq.

On Election Day 2004, US voters chose George W. Bush over John Kerry. This time, Bush won the popular vote as well as the electoral vote.

THE UNITED STATES AND SADDAM HUSSEIN

Saddam Hussein rose to power in Iraq during the early 1970s. In 1980, Iraqi forces invaded neighboring Iran. In the eight-year war that followed, the United States gave military aid to Hussein. US leaders thought Iran was a bigger threat to the United States than Iraq was.

By 1991, the situation had changed. When Saddam Hussein's troops invaded Kuwait, President George H. W. Bush acted quickly to force them to leave. Some Americans discussed forcing Hussein from power at that time, but the president said no.

After the war, US and British planes continued to patrol the skies over northern and southern Iraq to prevent Hussein from sending his military forces into those areas. Now Hussein saw the United States as his major enemy.

When the United States invaded Iraq in March 2003, Saddam Hussein escaped from Baghdad. US forces searched for him for months, sometimes coming within minutes of capturing him. Finally, in December 2003, an Iraqi citizen led US forces to a farmhouse in the countryside. Saddam Hussein was found hiding in a **spider hole.** In 2005, he went on trial (pictured above) in Iraq for "crimes against humanity." He was convicted and then executed for his crimes on December 30, 2006.

CHAPTER FOUR

DIFFICULT YEARS

On January 20, 2005, George W. Bush was sworn in as US president for the second time. Several days later, Iraqis voted in their first free election. President Bush praised the voting.

Although the war in Iraq took most of Bush's attention, he also had plans for new programs in the United States. Early each year, the president gives a speech, called the "State of the Union," in which he outlines his ideas for the coming year. In his 2005 State of the Union speech, Bush called for major changes in Social Security. The Social Security system was started in 1935.

Two Iraqi women cast their votes at a polling station east of Baghdad in 2005.

George W. Bush has always believed in going to bed early—usually before 10 p.m. On the night of his second inauguration, he raced through nine parties so he could get to bed at his regular time.

Under this system, workers pay a Social Security tax, which is used to provide money to the elderly, the disabled, and children who have lost their parents. Over the years, Social Security became a major source of income for workers after they retired from their jobs. But by the 21st century, some people worried that Social Security was in trouble. They said that the program would not have enough funds to pay all the Social Security money owed to Americans.

George and Laura Bush dance at a ball on the night of his second inauguration.

President Bush called for a new system that would let workers decide for themselves what to do with the money they paid into Social Security. This would give them the chance to earn more than the amount they would receive from Social Security. But they also risked losing money if the economy did not do well. Bush's idea was called **privatization.** Democrats resisted the privatization of Social Security. They worried that the elderly might not have enough money to live on if their investments did poorly. In the months that followed, they successfully defeated Bush's efforts to change the system.

As 2005 went on, Iraq continued to dominate the news. But the United States was also increasingly concerned about Iraq's neighbor, Iran. Iran wanted to build nuclear power plants to provide energy. The plants, however, could also produce material for nuclear bombs, the most destructive weapons in the world. Bush feared Iran could one day make nuclear weapons and use them to strike Israel, a US ally. He also feared that the Iranians might give nuclear weapons to terrorists. Bush said he wanted to use diplomacy to convince Iran not to build nuclear weapons. But later he stressed the United States was prepared to use force if Iran went ahead with building the weapons.

Presidents give a State of the Union speech before Congress each year. The speech outlines their goals for the future. In earlier times, some presidents sent written messages to Congress. In 1947, Harry Truman became the first president to deliver a State of the Union speech on television.

New Orleans residents wade through chest-deep floodwaters following Hurricane Katrina. The storm killed more than 1,200 people and did more than $80 billion worth of damage.

In the summer of 2005, a natural disaster turned the country's attention away from global issues. On August 29, Hurricane Katrina roared ashore along the Gulf Coast of the United States. Hardest hit was New Orleans, Louisiana. About 80 percent of the city was covered by floodwaters, and more than 1,200 people died. Many Americans criticized the US government's response to the storm as slow and inadequate. Many people were trapped in New Orleans without food or water or any way to escape their flooded homes.

As relief efforts continued along the Gulf Coast, Iraq also filled the news. In October, Iraqis accepted a new constitution for their country. But fighting continued in Iraq. More than 800 Americans were killed in 2005, and almost 6,000 were wounded.

Hurricane Katrina forced hundreds of thousands of people from their homes. Four months after the storm, the population of New Orleans was less than half of what it had been before the storm.

Meanwhile, the war on terror was beginning to harm other countries' opinions about the United States. In 2004, reports had emerged that some US soldiers had tortured Iraqi prisoners. In 2005, new reports claimed that the United States secretly took prisoners to countries where they might be tortured. And hundreds of people captured in Iraq and Afghanistan remained at Guantanamo, a US military base in Cuba. Many people around the world complained about the treatment of the prisoners in Guantanamo.

To fight terrorism, Bush had also ordered a government agency called the National Security Agency (NSA) to listen in on the phone calls and read the emails of some Americans. The NSA was supposed to get permission from a special court before doing this, but the president told the NSA not to. Some people said that Bush and his advisers were breaking the law in order to fight the war on terror.

Thousands of protesters marched in Boston in 2007. They demanded an end to the Iraq War.

All the while, the situation in Iraq continued to worsen. Attacks by insurgents were rising. Baghdad often had electricity for only four hours a day. Although some Iraqis were trained as police officers and soldiers, many lacked the equipment they needed to fight. US soldiers still did most of the dangerous work.

As the fighting in Iraq continued, President Bush became less popular among Americans. Some Democrats called for pulling US troops out of Iraq. The war was the main issue in the 2006 election, when voters chose members of Congress. In November, Democrats took control of both the US House of Representatives and the US Senate for the first time during George W. Bush's presidency.

US Army soldiers take cover while under fire from insurgents in Baqouba, a city northeast of Baghdad. Years after the United States ousted Saddam Hussein, troubles in Iraq remained.

A National Guard soldier scans the US-Mexico border in Arizona in 2007. President Bush sent thousands of National Guard troops to help US Border Patrol agents manage checkpoints and look for people attempting to cross the border illegally.

In 2007, Bush sent 30,000 more troops to Iraq. This surge, or boost in troops, brought the total number of US forces in Iraq to more than 160,000. Bush hoped that the extra troops would help stop much of the violence.

Throughout 2006 and 2007, President Bush also had to devote himself to other issues. He continued to speak out against Iran and its possible efforts to build nuclear weapons. He also joined other world leaders in convincing North Korea to give up its plans to build nuclear weapons.

Illegal **immigration** was a major issue during Bush's second term. Many people from other countries were entering the United States to find work. They came to the United States without the legal papers that allowed them to be there.

The president sometimes argued with members of his own party over this issue. Bush thought the United States should help illegal immigrants who were already in the country to become legal US residents. Some Republicans wanted tougher laws that would send illegal immigrants back to their home countries. They also wanted to prevent other illegal immigrants from entering the United States. Bush agreed that it was important to keep new illegal immigrants out. In 2006, he approved plans to build a 700-mile (1,100 km) fence along the border between Mexico and the United States to prevent people from sneaking in. He also sent more guards to patrol the border.

As president, George W. Bush dealt with difficult issues such as immigration, the economy, and the environment. But he will most likely be remembered for his efforts to fight the war on terror in Iraq. Though

Americans did not always agree with his decisions, President Bush remained convinced that he had done the right thing. "I made the decision to lead," he said in 2007. "I know, I firmly believe, that decisions I have made were necessary to secure the country."

On January 20, 2009, Barack Obama was inaugurated as the 44th president of the United States. Bush departed Washington, DC, for his home in Texas. In the years that followed his presidency, Bush has taken time to enjoy hobbies like writing and painting.

George W. and Laura Bush wave before departing the US Capitol after attending the inauguration of Barack Obama.

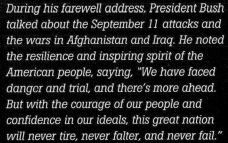

During his farewell address, President Bush talked about the September 11 attacks and the wars in Afghanistan and Iraq. He noted the resilience and inspiring spirit of the American people, saying, "We have faced danger and trial, and there's more ahead. But with the courage of our people and confidence in our ideals, this great nation will never tire, never falter, and never fail."

In 2010, he published a memoir, *Decision Points*, and in 2014, he released a biography of his father. In 2017, Bush released a book of his own portraits of veterans.

Bush has kept a relatively low public profile since his time in the White House. In 2010, at the request of President Obama, Bush joined with Bill Clinton to form the Clinton Bush Haiti Fund, raising support for survivors of the 2010 earthquake in Haiti. In 2012, he officially endorsed the Republican Party's nomination for president, Mitt Romney. Bush declined to endorse Donald Trump in 2016 and did not attend the Republican National Convention that year. Today, visitors can learn about Bush's life and presidency at the George W. Bush Presidential Library and Museum near Dallas, Texas.

TIME LINE

1940	**1960**	**1970**	**1980**	**1990**

1946
George W. Bush is born on July 6 in New Haven, Connecticut. His parents are George H. W. and Barbara Bush.

1948
The Bush family moves to Texas.

1964
Bush graduates from Phillips Academy in Massachusetts and helps his father during his campaign for the US Senate.

1968
Bush graduates from Yale University and enters the Texas Air National Guard.

1975
Bush earns a graduate business degree from Harvard University.

1977
In the summer, Bush meets Laura Welch, a school librarian. They marry in November.

1978
Bush runs for the US House of Representatives but loses.

1979
Bush starts Arbusto Energy, which he later renames Bush Exploration.

1980
Bush's father is elected vice president of the United States. Ronald Reagan is elected president.

1988
Bush's father is the Republican candidate for president. Bush helps run his campaign. In November, the elder Bush is elected the president of the United States.

1989
Bush and some business partners buy the Texas Rangers baseball team.

1994
Bush defeats Democrat Ann Richards to become governor of Texas.

1998
Calling himself a compassionate conservative, Bush wins reelection as governor of Texas.

2000
Bush wins the Republican Party nomination for president. The Democrats nominate Vice President Al Gore. The race is close, and the final result is decided in Florida. Arguments over the Florida vote end up in the Supreme Court. On December 12, the Court orders Florida to stop the recount of the vote, so Bush wins the Florida vote and the election.

2001
Bush is sworn in as president on January 20. On September 11, al-Qaeda terrorists strike the United States, killing almost 3,000 people. Bush vows to hunt down Osama bin Laden, the leader of al-Qaeda, and remove the Taliban, the leaders of Afghanistan who support him. US forces and their allies defeat the Taliban, but they do not find bin Laden.

2002
Bush and his advisers say Iraq has weapons of mass destruction and could share them with terrorists. Congress gives the president the authority to send troops to Iraq if he thinks the safety of the United States is being threatened.

2003
In March, US forces invade Iraq. Within a month, they oust Saddam Hussein. He flees but is later captured. In May, Bush declares that major combat operations have ended.

2004
Bush runs for reelection. He defeats Democrat John Kerry.

2005
Bush calls for the privatization of Social Security, but Congress opposes the move. Hurricane Katrina strikes the southern United States. New Orleans, Louisiana, is devastated. Iraq writes a new constitution. But insurgent attacks in Iraq rise, and Bush's popularity in the United States falls.

2006
The number of attacks in Iraq continues to rise. Some Democrats call for cutting American troop levels in Iraq. In the November elections, the Democrats take control of Congress for the first time during Bush's presidency. Bush calls for changes in immigration laws to help some illegal immigrants remain in the United States.

2007
Bush sends 30,000 more troops to Iraq in what is known as the surge. Bush joins other world leaders in convincing North Korea to give up its plans to build nuclear weapons.

2010
Bush releases his memoir, *Decision Points.*

2013
Bush undergoes surgery for a blocked coronary artery. All five living presidents attend the dedication ceremony for the George W. Bush Presidential Library and Museum, which opened later that year.

2014
Bush releases a biography of his dad. It is titled *41: A Portrait of My Father.*

2018
Bush's mother, Barbara, dies in April. His father, George H. W. Bush, dies in November.

2019
Bush's portraits of veterans are exhibited at the Kennedy Center in Washington, DC. The show is titled "Portraits of Courage" after his 2017 book.

GLOSSARY

allies (AL-lyze): Allies are people or nations who unite for a common goal. The United States and its allies forced the Taliban from power in Afghanistan.

ambassador (am-BASS-uh-dur): An ambassador is a person who represents his or her country in dealings with foreign nations. During the early 1970s, George H. W. Bush served as the US ambassador to the United Nations.

ballots (BAL-uhts): Ballots are the slips of paper or other items used to record votes in an election. During the 2000 presidential election, some ballots in Florida did not work properly.

campaign (kam-PAYN): A campaign is the process of running for an election, including such activities as giving speeches and meeting voters. George W. Bush worked on his father's campaigns before he ran for office himself.

candidates (KAN-duh-dayts): Candidates are people running in an election. George W. Bush was the Republican candidate for president in 2000 and 2004.

coalition (koh-uh-LIH-shun): A coalition is a group of nations united to fight a common enemy. President George W. Bush created a coalition to defeat Iraq in 2003.

communist (KOM-yoo-nist): A communist supports a system in which the government owns most businesses and runs the economy. The United States fought against communist forces in Vietnam.

conservative (kuhn-SUR-vuh-tiv): A conservative believes the government should play a small role in the economy and build a strong defense. George W. Bush called himself a compassionate conservative.

Constitution (kon-stuh-TOO-shun): A constitution is a set of basic principles that govern a state, country, or society. The US Constitution guarantees freedom of speech and other rights for Americans.

democracy (dih-MAH-kruh-see): Democracy is a political system with free elections. The United States tried to bring democracy to Afghanistan and Iraq.

diplomacy (dih-PLOH-muh-see): Diplomacy is the process of nations resolving differences in a peaceful way. In 2004, John Kerry said President Bush should have relied more on diplomacy before going to war with Iraq.

domestic (duh-MESS-tik): Events and issues linked to what happens within a nation are called domestic. George W. Bush believed tax cuts were an important domestic issue.

electoral votes (ee-LEKT-uh-rul VOHTS): Electoral votes are votes cast by representatives of the American public for the president and vice president. Each state chooses representatives who vote for a candidate in an election. These representatives vote according to what the majority of people in their state want.

hijacked (HY-jakt): Something that is hijacked is taken by force. In 2001, foreign terrorists hijacked four US planes and crashed them, killing almost 3,000 people.

immigration (ih-muh-GRAY-shun): Immigration is the act of coming to a new country to live. Illegal immigration became a major issue in President Bush's second term.

inauguration (ih-naw-gyuh-RAY-shun): An inauguration is the ceremony that takes place when a new president begins a term. At his first inauguration, Bush said he wanted to bring Democrats and Republicans together.

insurgents (in-SUR-junts): Insurgents are people who are fighting against the government. Iraqi insurgents committed thousands of attacks on US forces.

legislature (LEJ-us-lay-chur): The legislature is the lawmaking part of government. In 1972, George W. Bush thought about running for the Texas legislature but decided he needed more experience.

National Guard (NASH-un-ul GARD): The National Guard is a military group in each state that can be used by either the state or the national government. George W. Bush served in the National Guard.

nomination (nom-uh-NAY-shun): If someone receives a nomination, he or she is chosen by a political party to run for an office. In 2000, George W. Bush received the Republican presidential nomination.

political parties (puh-LIT-uh-kul PAR-teez): Political parties are groups of people who share similar ideas about how to run a government. The two major political parties in the United States are the Democratic Party and the Republican Party.

politics (PAWL-uh-tiks): Politics refers to the actions and practices of the government. Many members of the Bush family are involved in politics.

privatization (pry-vuh-tih-ZAY-shun): Letting private companies or individuals take over a government program is called privatization. In 2005, George W. Bush called for the privatization of Social Security.

spider hole (SPY-duhr HOLE): A spider hole is a round hole dug deep into the ground that is used as a hiding place. Saddam Hussein was pulled from a spider hole that was covered by a rug to hide the opening.

terms (TERMZ): Terms are the length of time a politician can keep his or her position by law. A US president's term is four years.

terrorist (TAYR-ur-ist): A terrorist is someone who uses violence and fear to force others to do something. Terrorists hijacked four planes on September 11, 2001.

treaty (TREE-tee): A treaty is a formal agreement between nations. George W. Bush pulled out of several treaties early in his presidency.

unconstitutional (un-kon-stih-TOO-shu-nul): If something is unconstitutional, it goes against the Constitution. In 2000, the Supreme Court said it was unconstitutional for the presidential votes to be recounted in only one Florida county rather than in the entire state.

United Nations (yoo-NYE-tid NAY-shunz): The United Nations is an international organization that includes almost every nation in the world. It was formed in 1945 to try to keep peace around the globe.

weapons of mass destruction (WEP-uhns of MASS di-STRUK-shun): Devices that can kill thousands of people at once are called weapons of mass destruction. In 2002, President George W. Bush feared Iraq would give weapons of mass destruction to terrorists.

welfare system (WEL-fayr SIS-tuhm): Government programs that help the poor, the sick, and the elderly are called the welfare system. President Bush supported reducing funds for the welfare system.

THE UNITED STATES GOVERNMENT

The United States government is divided into three equal branches: the executive, the legislative, and the judicial. This division helps prevent abuses of power because each branch has to answer to the other two. No one branch can become too powerful.

EXECUTIVE BRANCH

President
Vice President
Departments

The job of the executive branch is to enforce the laws. It is headed by the president, who serves as the spokesperson for the United States around the world. The president has the power to sign bills into law. He or she also appoints important officials, such as federal judges, who are then confirmed by the US Senate. The president is also the commander in chief of the US military. He or she is assisted by the vice president, who takes over if the president dies or cannot carry out the duties of the office.

The executive branch also includes various departments, each focused on a specific topic. They include the Defense Department, the Justice Department, and the Agriculture Department. The department heads, along with other officials such as the vice president, serve as the president's closest advisers, called the cabinet.

LEGISLATIVE BRANCH

Congress: Senate and the
House of Representatives

The job of the legislative branch is to make the laws. It consists of Congress, which is divided into two parts: the Senate and the House of Representatives. The Senate has 100 members, and the House of Representatives has 435 members. Each state has two senators. The number of representatives a state has varies depending on the state's population.

Besides making laws, Congress also passes budgets and enacts taxes. In addition, it is responsible for declaring war, maintaining the military, and regulating trade with other countries.

JUDICIAL BRANCH

Supreme Court
Courts of Appeals
District Courts

The job of the judicial branch is to interpret the laws. It consists of the nation's federal courts. Trials are held in district courts. During trials, judges must decide what laws mean and how they apply. Courts of appeals review the decisions made in district courts.

The nation's highest court is the Supreme Court. If someone disagrees with a court of appeals ruling, he or she can ask the Supreme Court to review it. The Supreme Court may refuse. The Supreme Court makes sure that decisions and laws do not violate the Constitution.

CHOOSING THE PRESIDENT

It may seem odd, but American voters don't elect the president directly. Instead, the president is chosen using what is called the Electoral College.

Each state gets as many votes in the Electoral College as its combined total of senators and representatives in Congress. For example, Iowa has two senators and four representatives, so it gets six electoral votes. Although the District of Columbia does not have any voting members in Congress, it gets three electoral votes. Usually, the candidate who wins the most votes in any given state receives all of that state's electoral votes.

To become president, a candidate must get more than half of the Electoral College votes. There are a total of 538 votes in the Electoral College, so a candidate needs 270 votes to win. If nobody receives 270 Electoral College votes, the House of Representatives chooses the president.

With the Electoral College system, the person who receives the most votes nationwide does not always receive the most electoral votes. This happened most recently in 2016, when Hillary Clinton received nearly 2.9 million more national votes than Donald J. Trump. Trump became president because he had more Electoral College votes.

THE WHITE HOUSE

The White House is the official home of the president of the United States. It is located at 1600 Pennsylvania Avenue NW in Washington, DC. In 1792, a contest was held to select the architect who would design the president's home. James Hoban won. Construction took eight years.

The first president, George Washington, never lived in the White House. The second president, John Adams, moved into the house in 1800, though the inside was not yet complete. During the War of 1812, British soldiers burned down much of the White House. It was rebuilt several years later.

The White House was changed through the years. Porches were added, and President Theodore Roosevelt added the West Wing. President William Taft changed the shape of the presidential office, making it into the famous Oval Office. While Harry Truman was president, the old house was discovered to be structurally weak. All the walls were reinforced with steel, and the rooms were rebuilt.

Today, the White House has 132 rooms (including 35 bathrooms), 28 fireplaces, and 3 elevators. It takes 570 gallons of paint to cover the outside of the six-story building. The White House provides the president with many ways to relax. It includes a putting green, a jogging track, a swimming pool, a basketball and tennis court, and beautifully landscaped gardens. The White House also has a movie theater, a billiard room, and a one-lane bowling alley.

PRESIDENTIAL PERKS

The job of president of the United States is challenging. It is probably one of the most stressful jobs in the world. Because of this, presidents are paid well, though not nearly as well as the leaders of large corporations. In 2020, the president earned $400,000 a year. Presidents also receive extra benefits that make the demanding job a little more appealing.

★ **Camp David:** In the 1940s, President Franklin D. Roosevelt chose this heavily wooded spot in the mountains of Maryland to be the presidential retreat, where presidents can relax. Even though it is a retreat, world business is conducted there. Most famously, President Jimmy Carter met with Middle Eastern leaders at Camp David in 1978. The result was a peace agreement between Israel and Egypt.

★ *Air Force One:* The president flies on a jet called *Air Force One*. It is a Boeing 747-200B that has been modified to meet the president's needs. *Air Force One* is the size of a large home. It is equipped with a dining room, sleeping quarters, a conference room, and office space. It also has two kitchens that can provide food for up to 100 people.

★ **The Secret Service:** While not the most glamorous of the president's perks, the Secret Service is one of the most important. The Secret Service is a group of highly trained agents who protect the president and the president's family.

★ **The Presidential State Car:** The presidential state car is a customized Cadillac limousine. It has been armored to protect the president in case of attack. Inside the plush car are a foldaway desk, an entertainment center, and a communications console.

★ **The Food:** The White House has five chefs who will make any food the president wants. The White House also has an extensive wine collection and vegetable and fruit gardens.

★ **Retirement:** A former president receives a pension, or retirement pay, of just under $208,000 a year. Former presidents also receive health care coverage and Secret Service protection for the rest of their lives.

QUALIFICATIONS

To run for president, a candidate must

- ★ be at least 35 years old
- ★ be a citizen who was born in the United States
- ★ have lived in the United States for 14 years

TERM OF OFFICE

A president's term of office is four years. No president can stay in office for more than two terms.

ELECTION DATE

The presidential election takes place every four years on the first Tuesday after November 1.

INAUGURATION DATE

Presidents are inaugurated on January 20.

OATH OF OFFICE

I do solemnly swear I will faithfully execute the office of the President of the United States and will to the best of my ability preserve, protect, and defend the Constitution of the United States.

WRITE A LETTER TO THE PRESIDENT

One of the best things about being a US citizen is that Americans get to participate in their government. They can speak out if they feel government leaders aren't doing their jobs. They can also praise leaders who are going the extra mile. Do you have something you'd like the president to do? Should the president worry more about the environment and the effects of climate change? Should the government spend more money on our schools? You can write a letter to the president to say how you feel!

> 1600 Pennsylvania Avenue NW
> Washington, DC 20500

You can even write a message to the president at **whitehouse.gov/contact**.

FOR MORE INFORMATION

BOOKS

Challen, Paul. *Surviving 9/11*. New York, NY: Rosen, 2016.

Edwards, Sue Bradford. *The Debate about the Electoral College*.
Mendota Heights, MN: Focus Readers, 2018.

O'Connor, Jim, and Ted Hammond (illustrator). *What Were the
Twin Towers?* New York, NY: Grosset & Dunlap, 2016.

Rauf, Don. *How George W. Bush Fought the Wars in Iraq
and Afghanistan*. New York, NY: Enslow, 2017.

Zahensky, Kenneth. *George W. Bush*.
New York, NY: Britannica Educational, 2018.

INTERNET SITES

Visit our website for lots of links about
George W. Bush and other US presidents:

childsworld.com/links

*Note to Parents, Teachers, and Librarians: We routinely verify our web links to make
sure they are safe, active sites. Encourage your readers to check them out!*

INDEX